Poison Pen Letters

Using the Mails For Revenge

by Keith Wade

Loompanics Unlimited
Port Townsend, Washington

POISON PEN LETTERS
©1984 by Keith Wade
Printed in U.S.A.

Published by:
Loompanics Unlimited
PO Box 1197
Port Townsend, WA 98368

Typesetting and layout by Patrick Michael
Cover by Kevin Martin

ISBN 0-915179-15-6
Library of Congress Catalog Card Number 84-81633

CONTENTS

Part I: The Individual
Waitress 7
Co-Worker 8
Mail Carrier 9
Dentist 10
Truck Driver/Delivery Person 11
Doctor 12
Corporate President 13
Taxi Driver 14
Bus Driver 15
Store Clerk 16
Law Enforcement Officer 17
College Student 18
Generic Mark 19
Painter 20
Janitor 21
Umpire 22
Private Detective/Generic Mark 23
Attorney 24
Landlord 25
Security Officer 26
Telephone Operator 27
Reporter 28
Union Officer 29
Teacher 30
Minister 31
Building Inspector 32
Mechanic 33
Social Worker 34
Electrician 35
Generic Mark 36

Part II: The Corporate Mark
Car Dealership 39
Manufacturing Company 40

Small Grocery Store 41
Department Store 42
Life Insurance Companies 43
Power Company 44
Funeral Home 45
Supermarket 46
Bookstore 47
Private School 48
Taxi Company 49
Water Department 50
Company Owned Gas Station 51
Privately Owned Gas Station 52
Airline 53
Printer 54
Movie Theater 55
Travel Agent 56
Radio Station 57
Railroad 58
Appliance Repair Shop 59
Newspaper 60
Credit Card Company 61
Bank 62
Church 63
Video Game Center 64
Amusement Park 65
Bar 66
Golf Course 67
Import and Export Company 68
Nursery 69
Farmer 70

Part III: The Government
Mayor 73
Senator 74
Representative 75
Aviation Administration 76
Business Administration 77
Social Security Program 78
Postal Service 79
Health Department 80
Jail Administration 81

Armed Services 82
Court System 83
Customs 84
Veterans Association 85
Police Department 86
Fire Department 87
District Attorney 88
Library 89
Coroner 90
Sanitation Department 91
Property Appraiser 92
Licensing Department 93
Department of Recreation 94
Public School System 95
Tax Collector 96
Department of Zoning 97
Animal Control 98
Highway Patrol 99
Division of Drivers Licenses 100
Clerk of Court 101

To Kathy McKinnon

ACKNOWLEDGEMENTS

I feel as though I should mention the following people:

My parents, for buying me the education necessary to write this book.

The other members of the family, who will most likely be offended if I don't mention them here.

The KMS.

Mr. Dick Kuhn, who probably knew that I'd do something like this.

Beth Horvath.

Scott Hurst, Kenny Clement, Bonnie Zane, Mary Susan Arosparger, Dick Prust and Susan Cieszko.

And Wilma Jean Brazelton, who probably wouldn't approve.

INTRODUCTION

The world is overpopulated with people who need to be hurt. However, those deserving such treatment are often too big, powerful, strong, or mean to be dealt with by mere mortals. Until now.

This book is the ultimate fantasy collection for those with a vengeful streak. It illustrates how even the giants can be brought down, safely. From the safety of a mailbox, they are dealt the revenge they so dearly deserve.

Consider yourself warned. This book was written and is sold for entertainment purposes only. Neither the author nor the publisher will take responsibility for your use of this book. The use of any of these letters will probably result in your being sued for defamation of character, libel, mail fraud, other damages, and copyright infringement. It is sold for you to laugh at. You assume the risk (and it is a great risk) if you choose to abuse this work.

There are a few things that a person should know before practicing the fine art of revenge by mail (including the name of a bailbondsman and a good attorney). Each and every typewriter has a distinctive type. A letter can be matched to the typewriter that it was created on every time. The bigger the mark, the more likely a postal investigation is. The Post Office does not think that mail fraud is very funny (some people have no sense of humor). Neither will a deserving mark. If you get caught, your attorney probably won't laugh either. Secondly, fingerprints *can* be lifted from paper. While the local dog catcher is unlikely to put much energy into finding out who you are, the President just might. Once again, the bigger the mark, the greater the danger.

The book is set up in three sections. The first illustrates how letters have been (and may be) used to deal with the individual mark. The second section illustrates how letters have been (and may be) used to deal with businesses that deserve this type of treatment. The third section illustrates how these letters have been (and may be) used to deal with the government. You will note that the United States government has not been dealt with in this book. This is not because these letters have never had their use there. Nor is it because the United States government is beyond reproach. Rather, it is because the wise man does not screw with the United States. The wise man does not even suggest it.

On the bottom of each letter the reader will find the name of the mark that the letter was used against. The person whose signature appears on the letter will have never seen the letter. This is called forgery. It works well. Ask a law enforcement officer what happens to a person who gets caught practicing forgery.

It is worthwhile to note that these letters could have been used for many purposes. I am not an idiot; I didn't reveal the exact facts in any of these letters. They've all been edited a little bit. With a little more editing, they could be used for countless marks. It has to be kept reasonable, however. If the people involved catch on, the plot will not work. If the mark catches on, the writer of the letter in question had better run for his life. In order to have the desired effect, some of these letters should be typed on the letterheads of the mark. Letterheads can be obtained by writing some kind of routine inquiry to the mark's office from a safe address. The mark will respond on his letterhead, and the letterhead portion of his reply can be cut off and taken to a print shop where many letterheads can be run off.

There is one other aspect that a person who intends to extract revenge by mail should be aware of. There is an important safety feature in a postmark. I can only be reached through a remailer. (KMIC, P.O. Box 444, Raeford, N.C. 28376, just in case you have some ideas for *Poison Pen Letters, Volume II*.) For a buck or so, a remailer will drop your stamped letter in a mailbox, giving you a postmark hundreds, or even thousands of miles away from your real location. KMIC is just one of the remailers in business; the Directory Of Mail Drops in the United States and Canada ($9.95 from Loompanics Unlimited) provides a comprehensive source of remailers.

One final note. All names and addresses found in this book have been made up. *Any similarity to any person, company, or organization, living, existing, dead or defunct, is completely coincidental.*

Enjoy!

—Keith Wade
August, 1984

PART I
THE INDIVIDUAL

WAITRESS

Jeanie Clausell
424 Nothingness Ave.
Mount Nowhere, N.J. 10076

February 1, 1984

Inspector
Mount Nowhere Health Dept.
Mount Nowhere, N.J. 10076

Dear Sirs,

I am writing this letter to let you know about a potential health hazard that exists in Mount Nowhere.

I have worked at the Mount Nowhere Drive-In Buffalo Restaurant for the last six years. My Christian upbringing has made it difficult to work there, but I need the money. I can not tolerate what is being done to the public any longer.

I have seen rotten meat scraped and served. Condiments are not refrigerated due to a lack of refrigeration space. I have asked the owner to fix the refrigerator, which often keeps meat no colder than room temperature, but he refuses. The kitchen is infested with roaches, and the exterminator can not control them. I am concerned with these things, but am unable to do anything about them.

I am sure that some of our practices are a violation of law. I sincerely hope that there is something that you can do about this.

Sincerely yours,

Jeanie Clausell

Mark: Jeanie Clausell, waitress.

Note: Send a copy of this letter to her boss in a health deparment envelope.

CO-WORKER

Miss Judy Gray
3424 S.W. 23 Court
Mount Baker, NM 23109

March 1, 1984

Mr. Randy Castlebran
President
Castlebran Manufacturing Company, Inc.
1 Grand Finale Concourse
Mount Baker, NM 23109

Mr. Castlebran,

I have been employed by your firm for the last three years. I am sure that you have no idea who I am.

Unfortunately, your supervisor, Mr. Kevin Jankil, does. Ever since I have been in his department, my job has been dependent upon my having sexual relations with him. When I threatened to tell you about this situation, he told me not to bother since "he knows what's going on."

I implore you to do something about this situation. I do not wish to quit because Mr. Jankil has informed me that by the time he is finished, no one in town will hire me.

Thank you in advance.

Respectfully yours,

Judy Gray

Marks: Judy Gray, Kevin Jankil.

Note: Send a copy to newspaper for additional mark: Castlebran Manufacturing Company, Inc.

MAIL CARRIER

Eduardo Smith
Mail Carrier

14 March 1984

Resident
19743 N.W. Easterly Blvd.
Flaredy, SD 23498

Dear Postal Patron,

I am sorry to inform you that I have misdelivered some of your mail. It was a mistake and I am very sorry for it.

The problem has now been cleared up.

You have __8__ pieces of first class mail at the local post office. If you would please pick them up, it would be a great help to us.

Thank you for your cooperation. Since the mistake was our fault, we are not charging you for holding this mail.

Sincerely yours,

Eduardo Smith

Mark: Eduardo Smith

DENTIST

RHC Marketing
1453 Julnim Street
Lynchburg, Tenn 23455

23 April 1984

Classified Advertising Editor
Lynchburg News
1 Main Street
Lynchburg, Tenn 23455

Dear Sir,

Please insert the following ad in the paper for the next week.

> Let the good times roll. 20 lb tanks nitrous oxide (for making your own whipped cream) $40.00. RHC Marketing, 1453 Julmin Street. Adults only.

Please find enclosed full payment for this.

Sincerely yours,

RHC Marketing

Mark: The dentist who practices at 1453 Julnim Street.

Note: There is no RHC Marketing, there's a dentist at that address. Call the local police and complain about your minor child acting crazy (i.e., light-headed, giggles, etc.). Indicate that he walks past the dentist's office on the way home from school.

TRUCK DRIVER/DELIVERY PERSON

E.G. Schrartz, Jr.
Schrartz's Quick Mart, Inc.
1200 Magnolia Blvd.
East Rockridge, Vermont 21455

15 March 1983

Mr. Ronald Tane
Tane's Florist and Gifts
325 N.W. 192nd St.
New Ridgeport, RI 21400

Dear Mr. Tane,

On 10 March 1983 at approximately 0800, one of your trucks pulled into our parking lot. The driver purchased 2 packs of potato chips, 2 six packs of Coors Beer, and a newspaper.

He claimed to have lost his wallet. Since he was driving one of your trucks, I decided to let him have it on credit. I do not expect you to pay for these items, but I would like some help.

The truck had the number 17 on the side. I would like to know who was driving it that day so that I can collect. He was there at least an hour, as he finished everything that he had purchased and threw away his trash. He seemed to be a nice enough person.

Any help that you can provide in this matter will be greatly appreciated. I hate to involve the police in a matter that I may be able to solve myself.

Respectfully yours,

E.G. Schrartz, Jr.

Mark: Driver, Truck 17.

DOCTOR

J. Foderingham Jaslow
Publisher
Young Lust
9701 N.W. 22nd Ave.
New York, New York 10022

December 9, 1983

New York District Attorney
New York, New York 10022

Dear Sir,

Recently, a local doctor, Mr. J.K. Creel III, offered to sell me some photos that he had taken of some of his female patients. I am not ratting on Dr. Creel. In fact, I shall not testify if called to court. I would, however, like the answers to some questions.

1. May I purchase photos taken with the consent of the patient?
2. May I purchase photos of adults taken without their knowledge?
3. How can I protect myself by making sure that the subjects are actually adults?

Your answer to these questions shall be most welcome. I am an honest publisher, who wishes to continue to operate within the law. My own attorney suggested that I contact you to be certain that any actions taken by me were lawful.

Most sincerely yours,

J. Foderingham Jaslow
Young Lust

Mark: Dr. J.K. Creel.

CORPORATE PRESIDENT

Robert Y. Kilcultyun
President
New Miami Fork Corporation
10000 Biscayne Blvd.
Miami, FL 33165

14 January 1984

Kelly O'Quigney
President
O'Quigney Auction Company, Inc.
2732 N.W. 17th St.
Miami, FL 33162

Dear Mr. O'Quigney,

I have been referred to your firm by a most reputable acquaintance. It is for this reason that I trust you with this matter.

It is necessary that the New Miami Fork Corporation liquidate seven million dollars worth of its stock. I feel that an auction would be most suitable and profitable way to do this.

If you would come to our plant on January 23 at 9:00AM, I should be pleased to work out the details with you. It is important that you come on this date as I am leaving for an international buying trip.

Sincerely yours,

Robert Kilcultyun

Mark: Robert Y. Kilcultyun.

Note: Write to Mr. Kilcultyun offering to sell very cheap merchandise only on January 23 at 9:00 AM. Call the chairman of the board and tell him that it's urgent that he be at the New Miami Fork Corporation at 9:00 AM on January 23.

TAXI DRIVER

Greenwich-Sansevereck Taxi Company, Inc
4652 Linwood Drive
East Grego, ND 20745

14 April 1984

North Dakota Department of Licenses
141 Regency Ave.
Haymont, ND 20712

Dear Sir,

This letter is in reply to the arbitrary drivers license suspension of one of my drivers, Mr. Peter F. Idziorek, Jr. I do not feel that this suspension was warranted.

You certainly know all of the details of this case. I do not believe that Mr. Idziorek was drinking at the time. My employees have too much respect for our cabs.

I am therefore requesting a hearing on Mr. Idziorek's request. I am willing to testify on his behalf as a character witness. I would appreciate a subpoena, however, for insurance purposes. (You know how insurance companies are; they won't pay for the time unless they have a copy of the subpoena, even though it's covered in the policy.)

Please feel free to contact me if I can be of any help in this case.

Sincerely yours,

Leo Greenwich,
President

Mark: Peter F. Idziorek, Jr.

BUS DRIVER

Jeffrey Manresa
Employee #2498, South Neyra Public Transportation Authority
530 Douglas Road
South Neyra, NM 13654

January 19, 1984

South Neyra Public Transportation Authority
City Hall
South Neyra, NM 13654

Gentlemen,

I have only been driving a bus for South Nerya for a short time, and am unaware of some of our policies. Therefore, I need some guidance.

On January 17, 1984, I found a paper sack in my bus. This sack contained $2564. I do not know what to do with it.

If you would please assist me in this matter, I should be most grateful.

Sincerely yours,

Jeffrey Manresa

Mark: Jeffrey Manresa.

STORE CLERK

Isador Breig
226 Circle Ter.
West Bregstein, Ill 64203

April 2, 1984

Mr. R.F. Bravo, Sr.
President, Bravo's 8th Street Fashions
4925 Main Street
West Bregstein, IL 64203

Dear Mr. Bravo,

I have worked in your 32nd street store as a sales clerk for the past 3 months. I have a problem that I'm not quite sure how to handle.

My supervisor, Mrs. Chilkes, has been stealing clothing ever since I came to work here. Since she is my superior, I have been unable to do anything about it.

Things are too expensive and I work too damned hard for my pay to allow this to happen. I implore you to do something about this. I remain willing to help you in any way to end this shocking situation.

Sincerely yours,

Isador Breig

Mark: Isador Breig.

LAW ENFORCEMENT OFFICER

Sgt. Mike Johnscraft
Yippieville Police Department
Yippieville, ND 20875

March 22, 1984

Editor
The Bloody News
Yippieville, ND 20875

Dear Sir,

I am appalled by the apparent attitude of your paper that the police of this town are lazy, inconsiderate, bigots who do nothing when they aren't beating up on the citizens.

Let me set the record straight. The police department of this town does a damned fine job considering what (or, perhaps, who) they have to work with.

A good majority of the people who live in Yippieville are slimebags. Those that do have the foggiest idea what is going on don't give a damn. For the most part, they are rude, inconsiderate, and have little or no respect for the law.

Then we have the mayor. He is a spineless administrator who is afraid to hire decent law enforcement. He is playing politics with the police department.

So, before you criticize, try to see things from our point of view.

Sincerely yours,

Sgt. Mike Johnscraft

Mark: Sgt. Mike Johnscraft.

Note: This letter must be printed by the paper to work. Keep it believable, printable, and reasonable enough that it won't be verified.

COLLEGE STUDENT

Irving Selzer
Warden
Chantilli State Prison
Tulsa, OK 23675

January 12, 1984

Dean of Students
Florida State University
Gainesville, FL 33165

Dear Sir,

Oklahoma state law GS-875 requires that the warden of a correctional facility make a reasonable effort to return any property left by former residents. In addition, if such property is valued at over $50.00, the warden must take exceptional steps to locate the former resident.

We have reason to believe that a Bart McComas is attending your school. Mr. McComas has ignored my letters to this point.

This is why I am writing to you. If you would please inform Mr. McComas that we simply wish to return his clothes, I would be most grateful. I do not blame him for being bitter with me since his last 6 months in our facility were spent in solitary confinement. However, I have a job to do, and the law requires that I return his belongings, even if he does make himself hard to find.

Thank you for your cooperation in this matter. If I can be of any assistance to you, please contact me.

Respectfully yours,

Irving Selzer,
Warden

IS/jj

Mark: Bart McComas, College Student.

GENERIC MARK

Jimmy Rhodens
316 Sleeping Rock Road
Whispering Siren, New Mexico 23467

March 21, 1984

Editor
The Whispering Siren Times
1 Whispering Siren Blvd.
Whispering Siren, NM 23467

Dear Sir,

How Dare You! How could you possibly omit an obituary? How would you like it if no one came to your funeral?

On March 20, 1984, I put my great aunt Chief Running Flower's obituary in your paper. I even enclosed payment in full. You, however, neglected to run the obituary.

My aunt Running Flower will be buried at 10:00 tomorrow at the Whispering Siren Memorial Resting Place. I would appreciate it greatly if you could make up for your stupidity and run the obituary like I paid you to do.

Sincerely yours,

Jimmy Rhodens

Marks: Jimmy Rhodens; Chief Running Flower Rhodens; The Whispering Siren Times.

PAINTER

J. Miller
Miller's Painting and Home Repair
5600 LeJeune Road
Jillman, Kansas 43009

April 3, 1984

Editor,
New Horizons Daily Times
1 Market Square
Jillman, Kansas 43009

Dear Sir,

I feel as though your readers should be involved in active protection of their children. It is for this reason that I write this letter.

I have been a painter for 15 years. I know just about all there is to know about paint.

Kilcutta Paint, Inc., a large and relatively new firm, makes a super product. It is, however, dangerous to children. The paint peels easily, and has a dangerously high lead content. It should not be used in homes that have children.

Sincerely yours,

J. Miller

Mark: J. Miller.

Note: Send a copy to the women's magazines, and, of course, Kilcutta Paint, Inc.

JANITOR

Jose Delmano
Jones Janitorial Service
2000 S. Ilking Street
Smithfield, NM 72118

January 29, 1984

Mr. Roger Tillman
President
Tillman Holdings, Inc.
1200 Springfield Ave.
Smithfield, NM 72118

Dear Sir,

This is really none of my business, but I feel as though it may be of some help to you.

Your image sucks. I would never invest in one of your projects. The office says a lot about a man, and yours indicates to me that you are a slob.

Other people see this office. It is the first impression that they have of you. Having seen your office, I have no desire to meet you; I don't associate with swine.

Please try to clean up your act.

Sincerely yours,

Jose Delmano

Mark: Jose Delmano.
Note: Although this is effective, it is *much more* effective if you can leave it on Mr. Tillman's desk.

UMPIRE

N. Kevin Gilmone
Umpire, Brasley Little League
1400 S. Park Drive
Brasley, VT 32999

5 April 1984

Mr. Jim Zire
Coach, Brasely Braves
234 Gilmort Drive
Brasley, VT 32999

Dear Sir,

In response to your horrible behavior at your last game, I issue this warning.

Little league is supposed to be a learning experience for our children. They are supposed to be learning how to be good citizens, not animals. I would appreciate it if you could keep this in mind.

I will not tolerate such behavior in the future. I will not fail to remove you if it occurs again.

It may be a tremendous request, but try not to be an ass.

Respectfully yours,

N. Kevin Gilmore

Mark: N. Kevin Gilmore.

PRIVATE DETECTIVE/GENERIC MARK

Linsome, Bransley, Frisco, and Dlers
Investigators Superior, Inc.
P.O. Box 23422
Key Biscayne, FL 33167

May 8, 1984

Mr. G.L. Provisly
231 S. Preston Street
New Retling, Ala 14321

Dear Sir,

We have accomplished our mission as requested. The substance was planted as per your instructions. Rest assured that Mr. Hilkes shan't see daylight for several years.

We are now requesting the remainder of our payment. If your satisfaction has been met, please remit our payment in the form of a check to cash at once.

It was a pleasure doing business with you.

Sincerely yours,

L.K. Linsome

Mark: L.K. Linsome.

Note: Misdirect this letter so that it goes to some honest person who thinks that dope plants by P.I.'s are humorless enough to involve the police in.

ATTORNEY

Harvey H. Jules, Esquire
Jules, Jules, Bradley and Tooles, P.A.
Madison Building, Suite 1000
Tulsa, OK 23111

April 5, 1984

Mr. R.J. Sperry
1200 N.W. 12th St.
Hollywood, FL 33166

Dear Mr. Sperry,

This is to inform you that your share in the estate of M. Spielburger has been recovered by our office.

We shall be pleased to forward your check upon receipt of our $150.00 fee for finding and securing this money due you.

Please remit our payment at once, and notify us of the mode of payment that you wish us to use.

Respectfully yours,

Harvey H. Jules

Mark: Harvey H. Jules.

Note: The more of these you send, the deeper the trouble for Mr. Jules. Be sure that the Oklahoma Bar and Attorney General get a copy or three.

LANDLORD

J.L. Wilson
Landlord
Wilson Manor
1267 N. Ocean Drive
Delnay, CA 19322

May 19, 1984

All Gone Exterminators, Inc.
2145 S. 72nd Ave.
Delnay, CA 19322

Dear Sir,

I would like to have you fumigate our 1-story, 56-unit apartment complex on June 15, 1984. The total area is 75,000 square feet.

I am making this request this far in advance because I am to take an extended vacation next Friday and the tenants have already been advised that they will have to vacate the week of the 15th.

If you have any questions, please contact me at the Hilton in south Paris.

Most respectfully yours,

J.L. Wilson

Mark: J.L. Wilson.

Note: The tenants should find this almost as amusing as the mark does.

SECURITY OFFICER

D.F. Lawrence III
Chief of Security
College of Remedial Education
Mt. Darwin, SD 63222

2 February 1984

Firearms of America, Inc.
23 Central Blvd.
N.Y., N.Y. 10022

Gentlemen,

Please send the following items to me at the College of Remedial Education on an open account. Our normal arrangement is 2/10, net 20.

15 Colt M16A-1
3 Ingram M11

Thank you,

D.F. Lawrence III

Class 1 FFL 1-59-02-H4-15991
Class 3 ATF ID#4679

Mark: D.F. Lawrence III.

Note: The FFL numbers are phony. You might want to send a copy of this letter and a short note to BATF.

TELEPHONE OPERATOR

New South Telephone Company
1200 Rhodel Ave
Steers, GA 43211

January 17, 1984

Mr. T.L. Ploone
434 S. Stranlet Street
Hallas, GA 43198

Dear Sir,

In response to your abusive treatment of me on January 15, 1984, I have a few comments to make.

I am hired to handle your calls. I am not there for you to abuse. I will not take such abuse from you in the future.

If you wish to continue to have uninterrupted telephone service, I suggest that you treat the operators in a nicer manner. Otherwise, you should be prepared to suffer the consequences.

Most Sincerely Yours,

Sandra Likely
Operator 17

Mark: Sandra Likely.

Note: You might want to send several of these to your nastier acquaintances.

REPORTER

G.F. Newsome
The Daily News
1 News Square
Glaredon, PA 21343

March 1, 1984

Mr. Patrick Bob McQuigney
The Glaredon Times
1235 Rodchester Ave.
Glaredon, PA 21343

Dear Sir,

In response to your inquiry, I respond with the correct information.

1. My story on the internal corruption within the News was not censored. I decided not to run it on my own.

2. Our editor was not fired, he resigned due to personal problems.

3. Our editor is not, nor has he ever been, enrolled in a drug rehabilitation program.

4. Our editor is not addicted to any substance.

Your allegations are totally unfounded. I do not know where your information is coming from, but it is totally incorrect.

Most sincerely yours,

G.F. Newsome

Mark: G.F. Newsome.

Note: You might want to write a letter to the editor of the News questioning the Times' motivation for attacking the editor of the News. You might want to write one to the editor of the Times questioning the editor of the News' problem.

UNION OFFICER

H.G. Pillman
Treasurer
United Ball Bearing Stackers
1500 New Range Road
Billmont, CA 32111

14 May 1984

President
First National Bank of Billmont
343 Main Street
Billmont, CA 32111

Dear Sir,

In an effort to make more money for our union, I am forced to remove our money from your bank. This letter of notification is to assure that you have the funds ready.

Please draft a check to H.C. Pillman in the amount of the balance of our account. I am sorry that we can no longer deal with you.

Sincerely yours,

H.C. Pillman

Mark: H.C. Pillman.

Note: The district attorney and the membership of the United Ball Bearing Stackers, as well as the press, would probably like a copy of this letter.

TEACHER

Mr. Abdul Lama
7141 Ocean Drive
Key Largo, FL 33154

March 21, 1984

Mr. and Mrs. Morris Leonor Jr.
2731 Dixie Blvd.
Key Largo, FL 33154

Dear Mr. and Mrs. Leonor,

I am concerned about your son John. Never in my career of teaching have I ever run across a child with problems like his!

I am not a psychiatrist. After 10 years of teaching, however, I have developed the ability to recognize a mentally disturbed child. I believe that John is such a child.

I recommend that you seek professional help for your child at once. His behavior is far beyond the realm of destructiveness. I can offer no other solutions.

I sincerely hope that you take my advice and have John evaluated. He would be a fine little man were it not for his bizarre behavior.

Most Respectfully Yours,

Abdul Lama

Mark: Abdul Lama.

MINISTER

The Reverand Irvin Kontos
New Hidalgo Church of God
3124 NW 57 Ave.
Penley, Conn 29654

25 March 1984

Mr. Mark Coreless VI
Publisher
Gay Women in Love
925 SW 78th St.
Washington, D.C. 20324

Dear Mr. Coreless,

I do not approve of pornography. I feel that it goes against God's laws. I do not feel, however, that your work, Gay Women In Love, is pornography.

Rather, I feel that it acts as an informational tool. It is well written, and well illustrated. It is for this reason that I recommend it to those who ask me about lesbianism.

Do not feel that the religous world is against you. We are against pornographers. Your magazine is a public service, and I shall continue to recommend it to those with questions.

May God bless you.

Sincerely yours,

The Reverend Irvin Kontos

Mark: The Reverend Irvin Kontos.

Note: This letter will almost certainly be printed in the next edition of Gay Women In Love. Be sure to purchase a few copies for distribution to congregation members.

BUILDING INSPECTOR

Zibmabway Construction Company
12001 NE 138th St.
N. Serayder, CA 34211

May 23, 1984

Mr. Robert Monterlongo
Director, Building and Zoning
2756 S. Main Street
N. Serayder, CA 34211

Dear Mr. Monterlongo,

If you will call the Clerk of Court, you will find that I declared bankruptcy today. Since your office was responsible, I thought that I'd let you know why.

Your Inspector Jones didn't demand much at first. Only a few dollars now and then. The next thing I knew, we were installing a swimming pool in his back yard. That was not as bad as his latest demand. Unable to pay his extravagant fee, and unable to work without his inspection, I had no choice but to close and move elsewhere.

Thank you, sir, for allowing me to lose my life savings. You have a nice day now.

Sincerely yours,

Joe Zibmabway

Mark: Inspector Jones.
Note: There is no Joe Zibmabway nor Zibmabway Construction Company.

MECHANIC

Charlie Swanburg d/b/a/
Hot Rod Motor Repair
2433 Arvida Street
Glencoe, Ill 76444

January 26, 1984

Editor
Hot Rod Express
2300 S. Trunjey Street
Glenfield, CA 21101

Dear Sir,

I am the head mechanic and owner of Hot Rod Motor Repairs. I am writing this letter to advise your readers of a potential problem with the FODD product Flairmont.

As many might be aware, this product has a defective brake connection. The manufacturer has refused to recall the car. As a result, there are many people driving unsafe vehicles.

I urge your readers to either pressure FODD into fixing this product or having it fixed at their own expense.

Respectfully yours,

Charlie Swanburg

Mark: Charlie Swanburg.

Note: Make sure that the public relations department of the large auto manufacturer that you choose to name gets a copy of this letter.

SOCIAL WORKER

Alvin Manner
New Fretrey Department of Housing
1234 Commerce Street
New Fretrey, Idaho 54211

14 February 1984

Mr. Howard Perez
Perez Grocery
2311 Rovington Rd.
New Fretrey, Idaho 54211

Dear Mr. Perez,

Your building is located in an area that the Department of Housing is considering placing a low rent development on. To be perfectly frank, we usually do not pay what a building is worth.

I think, however, that I can help you. I have two youths that need jobs. If you could let them work for you (at just above minimum wage), I think that I could convince the board to locate its building elsewhere.

Please let me know at once if you think that we can help each other.

Sincerely yours,

Alvin Manner
Department of Housing

Mark: Alvin Manner.

Note: Send one of these to each retailer in the area, as well as the press.

ELECTRICIAN

Do Good Insurance, Inc.
12000 Lilly Lane
East Chavelock, VA 54211

May 18, 1984

East Chavelock Power and Light, Inc.
4231 Hodgeraf Road
East Chavelock, VA 54211

Gentlemen,

On April 2, 1984, Mr. Ray Unmiler had his truck burglarized. Mr. Unmiler is a licensed electrician doing business in south eastern Virginia.

This letter is in reference to Mr. Unmiler's claim. Among other things that were stolen were 5000 East Chavelock Power and Light meter seals. Mr. Unmiler claims that they were valued at 7 cents each.

Would you please verify the cost of these seals for us. Also, were they the property of Mr. Unmiler, or did they remain the property of East Chavelock Power and Light Inc?

Thanking you in advance.

Sincerely yours,

Do Good Insurance, Inc.

Mark: Mr. Ray Unmiler.

Note: Meter seals are used only by the power company (in most cases). The person with a large number of these seals will be suspected (and most likely accused) of tampering with meters.

GENERIC MARK

John Edwards
15297 N.W. 23 Ave.
Lyons Landing, GA 14321

25 March 1984

Mrs. Terry Newton
1297 Grand Pine Avenue
Coral Gables, FL 33156

Mrs. Newton,

Although I have never met you, I feel as though I know you through your son Frank.

I am writing you because I feel that someone must know the truth behind my death. To be perfectly frank, you are the only person that I can trust.

By the time you get this letter, I will be dead. Hopefully, it will look like natural causes. In actuality, it was a suicide.

I lived with your son for several years. I loved him. I couldn't bear to live without him. When he left me for someone who was half the man I am, it was all I could take. That is why I killed myself.

Please keep this our secret. I am insured, but they won't pay for suicide. Tell your son that I love him and forgive him.

Sincerely,

John

Mark: Frank Newton.

Note: This may be the ultimate revenge by mail. Who could disbelieve it? The idea for this letter was given to me by a good friend, Alan MacDonell. Thanks, Al.

Note: Timing is crucial. The date of postmark must correspond to death of "writer."

PART II
THE CORPORATE MARK

CAR DEALERSHIP

Consumer Advocate
The Daily News
Port Greyly, Ark 22109

15 March 1984

President,
All Right Motor Sales Company
140 Quail Drive
Port Greyley, Ark 22109

Dear Sir,

Your practices have been brought to our attention by a Mr. Mark Smith, who purchased a late model blue Buick in February.

His attempts to get you to honor your warranty have been useless. Your claims that you did not sell him the car are among the worst business practices that I have ever seen. If you do not promptly take care of this problem, we shall be forced to do an expose on your method of doing business.

The car is a 1978 Blue Buick Skylark, VID GM12-43-5565-67.

Thanking you in advance,

Mark: All Right Motor Sales Company.

Note: It might help if the Daily News didn't exist and the address was somewhere where you could pick up the reply and perhaps respond to it.

MANUFACTURING COMPANY

Three Aces Distributors, Inc.
1400 S Bay Street
Rapid Falls, Minn 21111

24 May 1984

KLZ Manufacturing Company
Kilridge, Florida 33122

Gentlemen,

As per your instructions, I returned the 250,000 pieces of your item #213. I have a receipt that shows that they arrived at your warehouse on the 15 of May.

My question is quite simple, where is our check? We waited two weeks before returning this crap, as you said that you wouldn't be able to return our money before that time. Please remit your payment at once; we need money too.

Sincerely yours,

Three Aces Distributors, Inc.

Mark: KLZ Manufacturing Comany.

Note: Item numbers and manufacturer's address can be found on most products. If Three Aces actually exists, it is an additional mark.

SMALL GROCERY STORE

Smitty's Grocery
1238 Main Street
Georgeville, Colorado 04332

March 14, 1984

Georgeville Power and Light Co.
300 S. 2nd Street
Georgeville, Colorado 04322

Gentlemen,

 On March 23 - 28 I will be having my store rewired. It will be necessary to have my power disconnected during this time.

I am writing you in advance in hopes that you can meet my schedule. I will be open until 9:00PM on the 22, and the electricians will be arriving at 7:00AM on the 23. If there is any way that you could disconnect the service between these times it would be easier on all concerned.

Thanking you in advance,

Ronald Smitty

Mark: Smitty's Grocery.

DEPARTMENT STORE

President,
Hamilton Department Stores, Inc.
Corporate Headquarters
Hamilton Department Stores, Inc.
New York, New York 10022

May 15, 1984

Mr. Ray McCairn
President
McCairn's Worldwide Manufacturing Co.
116 E. 5th Ave Bay 16
Chicago, Ill 54333

Dear Mr. McCairn,

I am sorry to inform you that our stores have decided to stop carrying your line. This decision has been made after long consideration and thought.

We are ceasing to carry your products due to their low quality, high price, and your slack service. We shall find a manufacturer with a policy that is more palatable to our company.

Please cancel all orders that have not been filled and submit your final bill at once.

Sincerely yours,

Hamilton Department Stores, Inc.

Mark: Hamilton Department Stores, Inc.

Note: You might wish to send one of these to each of the store's major suppliers.

LIFE INSURANCE COMPANY

New Hope Life Insurance Company
New Hope Life Building
West Palm Beach, FL 33144

May 23, 1984

Mrs. Robert Jorge
1200 S.W. 17th St.
Klinging, Ill 54211

Dear Mrs. Jorge,

I am very sorry to learn of your husband's death. I am even sorrier to inform you that we can not pay his $100,000 death benefit.

Our investigation has ruled that his death was a suicide. We even think that you might have been involved in his purchasing this extra insurance just prior to his death. Since we can not prove this, however, we have decided not to prosecute you.

Sincerely yours,

New Hope Life Insurance Company

Mark: New Hope Life Insurance Company.

Note: Mrs. Jorge was found in the daily obits, as the wife of a man who died. Her husband did not commit suicide, nor was he insured by New Hope. There are several nationwide quasi-newspapers that would make a nice story out of a copy of this letter.

POWER COMPANY

Consumer's Power and Light, Inc.
1500 Legion Road
Hialeah, FL 33145

January 19, 1984

District Attorney
Metro Dade Administration Building
Miami, FL 33169

Dear Sir,

This letter is in inquiry of the amount of help that your office is prepared to lend us in the prosecution of meter tamperers.

We have one electrician, All Florida Electrical and Cooling Systems, Inc., that is practicing this on a gross scale. It would be nice to do something about this.

Any help that you could give on this particular case would be most helpful. We really would like to put a stop to this.

Sincerely yours,

Consumer's Power and Light

Mark: Consumer's Power and Light.

Note: Make sure that you choose an electrician that is clean and rich, with a good reputation. It's the power company you're after, not the electrician.

FUNERAL HOME

Terro Funeral Home
1200 S. 51st Court
Romera Valley, Alaska 13222

June 12, 1984

Editor
Romera Valley Times
701 N.W. 210 St.
Romera Valley, Alaska 13222

Dear Sir,

It is a sad commentary upon our police department to note that incompetent people are hired to serve as police officers.

As a funeral director, I work closely with the police department's administration staff. One can only hope that the officers that are on the street are far more competent than those in the office.

I urge the people of Romera Valley to attend the city council meetings. It is here that the decisions to keep these people working are made. Let your voice be heard. Vote in competent administration while you still have the chance.

Sincerely yours,

George Terro,
Terro Funeral Home

Mark: Terro Funeral Home.

Note: See when the next time he gets a police escort for a funeral is.

SUPERMARKET

North Star Grocery Store
7600 S.W. 34 Ct.
Lingemont, Texas 12844

May 1, 1984

Southern Food Products, Inc.
209 S. Hayes Street
Ft. Worth, Texas 13977

Gentlemen,

Please be aware that we will be remodeling our store during the month of June.

Therefore, we need to have food shipped on the following schedule.

First week of June: None
Second week of June: 1/2 regular shipment, delivered at 10:00 PM Thursday.
Third week of June: None
Fourth week of June: Double Shipment, delivered at 5:00 AM Tuesday.

After June, we will resume our regular shipping schedule.

Sincerely yours,

North Star Grocery Store

Mark: North Star Grocery Store.

Note: Make sure that all of North Star's regular suppliers get a copy of the changes. It's more fun if each gets a slightly different timetable.

BOOKSTORE

Likely Story, Booksellers, Inc.
South Street Mall
Port Eyen, SC 43122

May 12, 1984

Jernigan County Literacy Council
6630 S.W. 50 Terr.
Port Eyen, SC 43122

Gentlemen:

Obviously, we're very interested in Literacy. We, however, are not completely selfless.

We would like to help your cause. If you'll mention us in your ads, here's what we'll do:
1. Furnish you with up to $500.00 worth of books.
2. Sell you books at a 35% discount.
3. Offer a 10% discount to anyone who finishes your course.

We want to see a more literate world too.

Sincerely yours,

Likely Story, Booksellers, Inc.

Mark: Likely Story, Booksellers, Inc.

Note: This is a good public interest story. Why not send the papers and TV stations a copy of this letter.

PRIVATE SCHOOL

Lakeview Private School
400 Lake Drive
Hollywood, Cal 00321

3 January 1984

Advertising Editor
Hollywood Daily Times
3200 S.W. Park Street
Hollywood, Cal 00322

Dear Sir,

Please run the following ad, with a small border around it, in Monday's paper.

Lakeview Private School is sorry to announce that it has lost its accreditation. We will, however, continue to provide the high quality of education that we have always provided. We are in the process of regaining our accreditation, so this situation is only temporary.

Please bill us.

Thank you.

Lakeview Private School

Mark: Lakeview Private School.
Note: This actually happened at my high school. The results were not funny. The administration has every intention of suing the guilty party, if they ever find out who it is.

TAXI COMPANY

Hollings Taxi Service
900 Falcon Street
Gentry, OK 03211

8 March 1984

Gentry International Airport
Gentry, OK 03211

Gentlemen,

This letter is to report abuse in the taxi systems at Gentry International.

There are several cab companies that are allowed to jump line by your attendants. Since I can not afford to pay their fees, I am forced to wait in line.

This special treatment is hurting my business. I am just a small company, with 7 cabs. I have to operate one of them myself, and just can't afford bribery.

I sincerely hope that you will do something about this situation.

Sincerely yours,

Bob Hollings

Mark: Bob Hollings; Hollings Taxi Service.

Note: The local papers and TV stations would probably like a copy of this. If you hint that Mr. Hollings is being intimidated, his denials will sound even better.

WATER DEPARTMENT

City of Jenkins Water Dept.
10 E. Eastridge Blvd.
Jenkins, Mich 31119

July 14, 1984

Manager
Caplan Apartments
740 N.W. 61 Ave.
Jenkins, Mich 31119

Dear Sir,

This is to inform you that your water bill is two months overdue.

Our previous notices have gone unheeded.

If you do not remit a check within three days, we shall be forced to discontinue your water service.

Thanking you in advance for your cooperation in this matter.

Sincerely yours,

Collections

Mark: City of Jenkins Water Department.
Note: You may want to send several of these letters. Try to pick recipients who will get hostile over being accused of not paying their bills.

COMPANY OWNED GAS STATION

Retail Store #4415
Syndicated Oil Ventures, Inc.
14th & 53rd Streets
Jacinto, Iowa 83445

2 March, 1984

Blixley Distributors, Inc.
Port of Iowa, Iowa 83445

Gentlemen,

I am in need of about 2500 gallons of each grade of gasoline a month to supplement our current deliveries. The brand of gasoline is relatively unimportant, so long as it comes on time.

If you are able to supply such a small amount, please send a contract to our store.

Thanking you in advance,

Manager
Retail Store #4415

Mark: Retail Store #4415.

Note: The following people would probably like a copy of this: Syndicated Oil Ventures (who probably wouldn't appreciate the humor); The papers (who probably wouldn't think that it is funny, either); Each of the other oil wholesalers in the area; The District Attorney.

PRIVATELY OWNED GAS STATION

Medowlark's Stop and Shop
2700 Central Highway
Port Wayne, AL 22133

15 May 1984

Lowland Oil Distributors, Inc
1400 S. Main Street
New Yadkin, AL 22131

Gentlemen,

As provided for in the terms of our contract, I am not going to renew our contract at its termination.

This change is due to your poor service and inflated wholesale prices.

This is your official notice as required in our contract. After the date of expiration, we wish to do no further business with you.

Sincerely yours,

Medowlark's Stop and Shop

Mark: Medowlark's Stop and Shop.
Note: This would have more credibility if it were sent certified, return receipt requested.

AIRLINE

Bob,

Your stuff is coming back to the United States in the same suitcase that we always use. It will be on Southern Airlines flight 332 on Monday, April 17.

I've got the cash. If you need any more shipments in the next month, I can be reached at the house in Buenos Aires.

Take care.

Mark: Southern Airlines.

Note: Customs and the FBI would probably like a copy of this. For additional mark, address the letter and/or sign it with the name of an enemy.

PRINTER

Howard Printers
16620 Marcel Blvd.
Corinne, Mass 31000

22 May 1984

Corinne Combined Charitable Operations, Inc.
1349 W. 39th St.
Corinne, Mass 31000

Gentlemen:

Having just recently become aware of your fine cause, I'd like to help you out.

I can't make a financial contribution; times are rough.

I will, however, take care of your printing - - gratis.

I'm sure that you'll be pleased with our service. Just drop your work off and we'll be glad to do it within 24 hours.

Respectfully yours,

Howard Printers

Mark: Howard Printers.

Note: This works best with a charity that uses a printer a lot. The local papers would probably like to hear of Howard Printers' generous offer.

MOVIE THEATER

Q.R. Molb
3015 N.W. 82nd Ave.
Rafhael, Nevada 10844

May 1, 1984

Modern Productions, Inc.
1 Modern Ave.
Hollywood, CA 20843

Gentlemen,

I just saw your latest release, Jarscharer, and it was great. I loved it!

My question is, why doesn't the Rafhael Theater get more of your first-run movies? This is the first new picture that they have had in years. I would really enjoy seeing more such movies at the theater.

Respectfully yours,

Q.R. Molb

Mark: Rafhael Theater.

Note: The Rafhael Theater has never shown Jarscharer. Since they haven't shown the movie, they haven't paid Modern Productions its royalty fee. Let's not tell Modern what happened though, okay?

TRAVEL AGENT

R.L. Grandon
Treasurer
First Church of Pedraza
1200 S. Linton Drive
Pedraza, NY 10021

January 12, 1984

The Pego Tour Co.
1320 S. W. 23rd Ct.
Pedraza, NY 10021

Gentlemen,

I would like for you to arrange a tour of Paris for 20 - 30 adults.

It would be preferable if the tour could last from 7 - 10 days. We would need to leave on April 17.

We need prices and itineraries as soon as possible. We are interested in the price range of $1700 - $2800 per person.

Thanking you in advance for your cooperation.

R.L. Grandon

Mark: The Pego Tour Company.

Note: This works better if a few promises (keep it reasonable) are made.

RADIO STATION

WEEL Radio, 98.6 FM
100 Jasco Street
Port Jaramillo, RI 73222

14 April 1984

Mr. J.H. Rayes
19667 Pine Circle
Port Jaramillo, RI 73222

Dear Mr. Rayes,

Congratulations!!! As you are well aware, WEEL has been running its Super WEEL contest for three months now.

It is my pleasure to let you know that you have won the WEEL Super Prize, a 1984 Ford Bronco II.

Please show up at Reynold's Superior Car Sales on April 26 to claim your prize. Be forewarned, we will ask you to say a few words, which will be transmitted live to our listening audience. Also, the press will show, so wear something nice.

Congratulations!

Jealously yours,

WEEL Radio

Mark: WEEL Radio.

Note: It may prove more fun to send these to several people. The press might be interested, if someone would call them.

RAILROAD

Friedenburg and Serranoville Railroad
Serranoville, KY 72009
Security Office

April 7, 1984

Janpol Department Store, Inc.
9800 N.W. 8th Ave.
Friedenburg, KY 72018

Gentlemen,

As I was driving by your store yesterday, I noticed your nice parking lot. The new paving really looks sharp.

I regret to inform you, however, that part of this pretty parking lot does not conform to railroad standards. As your deed clearly states, 250 feet of DIRT must exist between the railroad track and anything else. Your parking lot is not in compliance.

Please correct this problem within the next 72 hours, and we will not take this action to court.

Sincerely yours,

Friedenburg and Serranoville Railroad

Mark: Friedenburg and Serranoville Railroad.
Note: Certain store owners will get very hostile if they get such a letter. These are the ones that should get one. The more outrageous the demands, the more static they'll generate.

APPLIANCE REPAIR SHOP

Eugene's Refrigeration and Appliance Repair
1400 Oakeen Drive
Mt. Lacy, VT 65322

May 13, 1984

Frieder Appliance Manufacturing Corp.
1400 S. Rayson St, Bay 12
Detroit, Mich 49388

Gentlemen,

What happened to your quality control on your model 129 refrigerator? I've seen a dozen of them go out in the last week.

Obviously, I'm not complaining. I am, however, ordering more parts. I need 15 compressors for this unit as soon as possible (really, I need them sooner than that.)

Please ship the 15 by an overnight express service, and I shall remit your payment (including the extra (and probably outrageous) postage charge.)

Respectfully yours,

Eugene's

Mark: Eugene's Refrigeration and Appliance Repair.

NEWSPAPER

The Screaming Eagle Daily Times
1 Screaming Eagle Square
Clemente, NJ 61110

10 February 1984

Dean of Students
Clemente University
Clemente, NJ 61110

Dear Sir,

Our paper is conducting a survey. We are terribly interested in your opinions on chalk. If you will participate in our survey, we will be glad to say something nice about your school when we publish the results.

What brand of chalk do you prefer?
What color do you prefer?
How much chalk do you buy a year?
Where do you buy your chalk?
Are you concerned with the health hazards of chalk?
Where do you store your chalk when not in use?
Who has access to this chalk?

If you would answer these questions, and get some input from your faculty about chalk, we'd be most pleased. We really would appreciate some printable faculty opinions, also.

Sincerely yours,

The Screaming Eagle Daily Times

Mark: The Screaming Eagle Daily Times.

Note: The more questions that appear, the stupider the newspaper will appear. The other newspapers in town would probably like a copy of this. Special thanks to Dick Kuhn, who was partially responsible for the formation of this one.

CREDIT CARD COMPANY

Albert Godinez
1240 W. Euclid Ave.
S. Ralston, Tenn 44312

May 18, 1984

Modern Day Charge Company
4199 N.W. 25th St
New York City, NY 10022

Gentlemen,

Enclosed you will find my charge card. It is enclosed because of your poor method of doing business.

For 18%, you'd think that you could provide a little better service. This is not the case. My wife's card was stolen several weeks ago. Due to your inept operator, I have been declared responsible for $40.00 worth of charges that I did not make.

Therefore, I've enclosed my own card. I shan't carry a card whose issueist cares so very little.

Sincerely yours,

Albert Godinez

Mark: Modern Day Charge Company.
Note: Do *NOT* seal this letter. The mark will believe that the card got lost in the mail. The person who appears to have signed the letter should be a nastier type.

BANK

Ludovici School for the Blind
605 N.W. 118th St.
Ludovici, Tex 93221

April 7, 1984

Editor
The Ludovici Times
Ludovici, Tex 93211

Dear Sir,

I realize that this is neither the time nor the place to make an appeal. We have neither the time nor the resources to utilize the proper means.

We desperately need the help of your readers. The 3rd International Bank of Houston is about to foreclose on our building.

As you know, we are a non-profit organization that lives from day to day. We simply can not raise the remaining $7000.00 This is why we are appealing to your readers.

Please help us defeat this giant bank and prove that charity still exists.

Sincerely yours,

Ludovici School for the Blind

Mark: The 3rd International Bank of Houston.

CHURCH

First Michaelides Church of Reno
4450 S. Carnoto Blvd.
Reno, Nevada 52110

May 1, 1984

Reno City Council
Reno, Nevada 52110

Gentlemen,

It is a disgrace that business is conducted on the Lord's day. I am referring to the Hane Street Shopping Mall, that sits just one block from our church.

You are an elected group of officials. If you can not see fit to meet the people's needs, perhaps you need to be replaced.

I trust that this matter will be considered in the next coucil meeting. If it is not, you may find that you have attended your last council meeting.

Sincerely,

Senior Minister
First Michaelides Church of Reno

Mark: First Michaelides Church of Reno.

Note: Local newspapers and businesses might be interested in this letter.

VIDEO GAME CENTER

Fun City, Inc.
Nation's Largest Coin Operated Game Center
Corner of 5th and Main Streets
Galpin, Arizona 21000

July 5, 1984

Office of Counterfeit Money
Washington, D.C. 10022

Gentlemen,

This is in inquiry to the proper method of disposal of slugs. Like any game center, we get our share of them.

I have $45.00 face value of counterfeit quarters at this time. Can I sell them for use in my game room? Will you send an agent to pick them up, or must I send them to you? Being new in the business, I don't know what to do.

I await you reply.

Repectfully yours,

Fun City, Inc.

Mark: Fun City, Inc.
Note: There is no Office of Counterfeit Money, but there is a government agency that would be just as concerned.

AMUSEMENT PARK

Laff a Minute, Ltd.
Nation Wide Amusement Parks
Fernandez Building, Suite 100
Hollywood, CA 32999

June 4, 1984

Manager
Laff a Minute Park 43
Pardo, HI 21999

Greetings,

Our national inspection crew will be visiting your park on June 7, 1984. Therefore, it will be necessary for you to close from June 6 1984 to June 8,1984.

We know that this will be both a pain and costly. You can be sure that it is not our idea. It is by federal regulation that each park must be certified. We just do as we are told.

Looking forward to seeing you. Perhaps we can make this waste of time a little more profitable by discussing future plans.

Sincerely yours,

President
Laff a Minute, Ltd.

Mark: Laff A Minute.
Note: This is most costly on a three day, warm weekend.

BAR

Mazor Printing
555 Graham Street
Grand Caymen Island, The Bahamas 22011

June 3, 1984

Bureau of Alcohol, Tires, and Flares
Washington, D.C. 10022

Gentlemen,

As part of their promotion, Pedray's in Herrara, New Mexico has hired us to produce 5000 replica bottle seals. While these seals are to be used on souvenir bottles, they have requested them to look authentic.

If you would send us a replica of the Treasury Department's seal, as well as any other information that you think we might need, we'd be most grateful.

Sincerely yours,

Mazor Printing

Mark: Pedray's (local bar and grill).

Note: The foreign printer adds credibility. The government probably won't believe that these seals are to be used on souvenir bottles.

GOLF COURSE

Pomponio Country Club
Pomponio, Maine 22424

June 14, 1984

President
S. Pomponio Running Club
107 S.W. 47th St
Pomponio, Maine 22424

Dear Sir,

Are you aware of the maintenance costs of keeping up a golf course? They are high enough without your membership tearing up our course.

If you choose to run through our course, please follow the map that I have enclosed. You will not do any damage if you follow it.

I am a runner myself. I realize that you need a place to run, and I am more than happy to be able to let you run on our course, IF YOU FOLLOW THE MAP.

Sincerely yours,

Pomponio Country Club

enclosure

Mark: Pomponio Country Club.

Note: The map is available from the pro shop. Be sure to indicate the path of most destruction. This will also work with the nearby motorcycle clubs, etc.

IMPORT AND EXPORT COMPANY

Duhart Import & Export Corp.
100 S. Kutteroff St.
NY, NY 10022

15 May 1984

Duhart Import & Export Corp.
2300 Polint Dr.
Emmer, Korea

Management team,

This is confidential information. Be prepared to bail out. Get everything ready so that the entire crew can come home by the end of next week.

I can't tell you why, this is private information. I don't care what you tell the workers, but don't panic them. Don't mention a word about this, not even to me (who knows who's listening to our conversations?) Wind the show down and be ready to leave on my command.

Shred this letter.

Sincerely yours,

Ralph Duhart
President

Mark: Ralph Duhart's Duhart Import & Export Corp.

NURSERY

Geer Nursery, Inc.
245 Palmer Ave.
Faver, Mass 23000

January 13, 1984

City of Faver Water Dept.
4000 S. Main Street
Faver, Mass 23000

Gentlemen,

We are reworking our water system and will need our service disconnected by you on January 19, 1984, for a period of 72 hours.

Please consider this your authorization to disconnect the service. You are not authorized to reconnect the service until you hear directly from me.

Sincerely yours,

Geer Nursery, Inc.

Mark: Geer Nursery, Inc.
Note: This works best in the summer.

FARMER

United Beef Growers of Hanna Texas
Sheps Building, Suite 459
Hanna, Texas 63221

May 12, 1984

Dear Meat Manager,

It has always been our policy to let area supermarkets know about abuses that we are aware of. Part of our job is protecting the image of the beef growers of Hanna.

Because of the poor health standards of the ranch, we are urging you not to buy beef raised or handled by the Holcolmb Ranch of Hanna. While your cooperation is voluntary, it would be wise to consider our advice. Like you, we want the public to receive only the best quality beef.

If I can be of any help to you, please call me at 929-1002.

Sincerely yours,

United Beef Growers
Hanna, Texas

Mark: Holcomb Ranch.

Note: This can work well with any type of livestock. Each grocer, supplier and distributor would probably like their own copy of this letter.

PART III
THE GOVERNMENT

MAYOR

An Open Letter to the People of Murawski

Dear Population,

Taxes are too damned high! I feel the bite each time I make a purchase. I love each and every penny that I earn, and I hate to give them up.

I also note that our city needs more service. We are lagging behind in almost every area. This is why I am going to propose an extra 2% sales tax, increase personal property taxes by 7% and increase the city income tax by 7%.

These additional taxes may hurt. We have no other alternative. I urge each and every one of you to back me in this effort.

Respectfully yours,

Mayor E.J. Kichen

Mark: Mayor E.J. Kichen.

Note: The local newspaper will be more than happy to run this. Would you believe his denial?

SENATOR

E. J. Fairchild
963 N. W. 230 Ave.
Mexico City, Mexico 02101

13 April 1984

Postal Inspector
Mexican Postal Service
19 Plaza
Mexico City, Mexico 02101

Dear Sir,

I recently received an advertisement in a postage-free envelope. The advertisement was for a local used car lot, and the envelope said "Postal Franking, Senator Jack Cassidy." Unfortunately, I threw both the envelope and advertisement away.

My question is, can this senator use postal franking for such a purpose? I don't feel as though I should pay for his advertisements.

I await your reply.

Sincerely yours,

E. J. Fairchild

Mark: Senator Jack Cassidy.

REPRESENTATIVE

J. Glassburg
Your Elected Representative

Dear Voter,

As you know, it has long been my policy to save our nation money any time that I can. This is why I have been called Cost-Cutting Jim.

Well, once again I'm on the rampage. I have developed a plan that would save our country close to $7,000,000 a year.

As you know, the government maintains a fleet of vehicles. They are all made right here in this country. That's nice, but expensive.

That's why I'm recommending that as of July 1, 1984, the government not spend another penny on domestic automobiles. They're just too damned expensive! I will do everything within my power to pass a bill requiring the government to buy the less expensive foreign models.

I just wanted to let you know who was lowering your tax bill.

Respectfully yours,

Jim

Mark: Representative J. Glassburg.

Note: If these are sent to the right people, it is not necessary to send a large number of them. Newspapers, labor unions, television stations, and other such sources make good distribution networks.

AVIATION ADMINISTRATION

J. L. Schrek
Schrek's Cafe
580 Ferris Ave.
Paris, France

14 June 1984

French Aviation Administration
1229 Coral Lane
Paris, France

Gentlemen,

This letter is an inquiry about the new flight plans being used by Fiedler Airlines, Inc. I would like to know why you have authorized the flight of jumbo jets so low over a commercial area.

I called about this, and you said that they were not flying over my cafe. I know that they are, because the few customers that still come into my cafe (the rest do not like to eat on a running strip, which is what you have turned my cafe into) complain about the noise.

I beseech you to do something about this problem.

Sincerely yours,

J.L. Schrek

Mark: French Aviation Administration.

Note: Fiedler Airlines is not flying over the area. Mr. Schrek's letter would be more impressive if it included a few affidavits from his "customers."

BUSINESS ADMINISTRATION

Dr. L.P. Allen
University of Switzerland
Marinis, Switzerland

18 March 1984

Swiss Business Administration
1640 Taylor Street
Prurtz, Switzerland

Gentlemen,

I would very much like for one of your small business experts to address my class on 2 April 1984. We would need you to arrive by 10:00 AM.

You can speak on anything that you'd like. Starting and running a small business is the general theme of the course.

Of course, the University will reimburse you for any expenses that you incur due to the trip.

Respectfully yours,

Dr. L.P. Allen

Mark: Swiss Business Administration.

Note: Both the college and the Swiss Business Administration should be rather surprised.

SOCIAL SECURITY PROGRAM

Dictatorship of Uganda
Department of Social Security
Government Center
Mears, Uganda

May 18, 1984

Dear Social Security Recipient,

It is with great regret that we inform you of a general cut in social security benefits. These cuts are over-all and will affect everyone.

Effective July 1, 1984, your benefits will be reduced by 18%. Your check will reflect this change.

Sincerely yours,

Mark: Dictatorship of Uganda, Department of Social Security.

Note: While there are a few elderly people that would raise hell about this, it would just unfairly upset most. For this reason, the newspapers, senior citizens groups, and TV stations make the best recipients of this letter.

POSTAL SERVICE

Hungarian Postal Service
Encapara

8 July 1984

Rothenburg & Rothenburg, P.A.
2539 Cleveland, Suite 323
Sullivan, Rafuse

Gentlemen,

This is to inform you of charges pending by the Hungarian Postal Service against your firm.

You will appear in our headquarters, with all mail received by your firm over the last year, at 8:00 AM on Monday, 16 July 1984. Your failure to do so will result in a judgement being issued against you.

If you have any questions, you may call 921-0034 between 9:30 AM and 1:00 PM Monday through Friday.

Sincerely yours,

Mark: Hungarian Postal Service.

Note: This works best if a powerful person receives this letter. The phone number is some pay phone somewhere.

HEALTH DEPARTMENT

Health Department
County of Muransky
6300 SW 23rd Ct.
Robins, NJ 40544

2 April 1984

Mr. J.H. Elliot
4500 Hilcrest Dr
Robins, NJ 40544

Dear Mr. Elliot,

Enclosed you will find a strip of bacon similar to those that are being sold in local supermarkets. We have reason to believe that it is a potential health hazard.

If you would please sample it (feel free to prepare it to your liking) and let us know about any ill effects that you suffer, we would be most grateful.

We have chosen you for this project because your family and friends have indicated that your life is of little value anyway.

Yours in a patriotic way,

Mark: Health Department.

Note: This letter seems outlandish. I pulled it on a friend, Mr. Willy Joe Quigney, to see if it would work. It did. Thanks for being my field tester, Joe.

JAIL ADMINISTRATION

Mecklinger's Fine Food
Corner of 4th and 19th Streets
Republic of Guam

14th May 1984

Editor
Guam Sunrise News
1400 S. Juliano Ave.

Dear Sir,

Once again you have run an editorial criticizing our government without offering any solutions. I think that I can provide a method of cutting some expenses.

For the last several years I have been purchasing surplus food from the Guam Detention Center on N. 48th Court. It is good food — too good. It is by far superior to any food that I can buy on the open market. The cuts of meat are better and the vegetables are fresher.

This is a waste of money. Why should society's scum be eating the same food that is served in the finest restuarant in the Republic? It would save a lot of money to cut down on quality. I don't see why prisoners should eat better than my family does.

Sincerely yours,

Mark: Guam Detention Center.

Note: The attorney general would probably be interested in this food selling scam. The warden will, of course, deny it. If you were selling government owned food, wouldn't you deny it? Too bad that he isn't.

ARMED SERVICES

South African Department of Defense
Department of the Army
100 S. Micele St.
Connell, Sabbah

22 May 1984

Khayta Mobile Home Complex
2567 Hindl Blvd
Jarvis, Rudich

Gentlemen,

We are prepared to offer you $25,000 for your property. We feel that this is a fair offer.

If you choose to accept it, please contact us within 7 days.

If we have not heard from you within 7 days, we will start condemnation procedures in District Court.

Respectfully yours,

Mark: South African Department of Defense.
Note: Everyone within 2 miles of the closest base, as well as local newspapers, should get a copy of this.

COURT SYSTEM

Judge G.L. Hartley

25 April 1984

Clerk of Court
Pietter County Courthouse

Dear Sir,

It has become necessary to have some of the records of my cases delivered to Washington, D.C. I need your help, and I need it at once.

Please deliver a photstatic record of my transcripts to 3800 S. Ocean Drive, Washington, D.C. 10022, by 28 April 1984.

Sorry about the short notice, but it wasn't my idea.

Respectfully yours,

Gary

Mark: Pietter County Court System.

Note: The bigger the system, the more expensive this letter will become.

CUSTOMS

Department of Customs
Commonwealth of Porazzo

19 May 1984

Porazzo International Airport
Porazzo

Gentlemen,

As you are well aware, our office in your terminal is hardly adequate. For this reason, we wish to remodel it. The government has allocated $350,000 for this purpose.

This project will start on June 1, 1984. We would appreciate it if you would allow us to use another location and route all traffic through this location starting this date.

Your cooperation is greatly appreciated. We are sure that you will be as pleased with our new look as we will be.

Respectfully yours,

Mark: Department of Customs, Commonwealth of Porazzo.

Note: This works much better if the person who "signs" the letter is a high ranking Customs official with the power to do this.

VETERAN'S ASSOCIATION

Dutch Veteran's Association
3030 Lakewood Lane
Lefwoitz, Holland

9 April 1984

Dutch Veteran's Association Chapter 34
7550 Hillcrest Rd.
Quailtance, Holland

Gentlemen,

The Dutch Veteran's Association maintains a sterling image. We represent our country and our fighting men. We mustn't let this image become tarnished.

Due to the recent actions of your Executive Director, we have decided to suspend your organization. You have become a discredit to our name.

Members are free to go to local chapters during this time. You will be at home there, just as you were in your own chapter.

Respectfully yours,

National Director

Mark: Dutch Veteran's Association.

Note: A similar organization (right here in our own country) that is supposed to have similar causes screwed over a friend of mine. Their letter wasn't quite as harsh as the one above. It brought an influx of membership cancellations, however.

POLICE DEPARTMENT

Three Star Security, Inc.
2436 Van Burean St.
Fisher, SD 34077

20 May 1984

Mayor
Fitterling, SD
Fitterling, SD 70744

Dear Sir,

We are most upset to hear of the resignation of your chief of police. From what we read in the papers, he was a good man.

He has applied for a job as Chief of Security with our firm. He has informed us that you would recommend him. If you would send your letter within the next two weeks, it would really help us out. I would hire him today, but our investors want more proof.

Respectfully yours,

Three Star Security, Inc.

Mark: Fitterling Police Department.

Note: This is more effective if several letters from different companies arrive. This was accidentally inspired by Tom Goodwin. Thanks, Tom.

FIRE DEPARTMENT

Commander
Etcovitch Fire Department
1971 SW 39th St.
Etcovitch, KY 50034

19 April 1984

Etcovitch Department of Maintenance
20 Main Street
Etcovitch, KY 50034

Greetings,

As you are probably well aware, the Governor's Council for Efficiency is touring our petty little city in order to balance the budget of Kentucky. We are, of course, the reason that this great state is $4 million in the hole.

In any event, they have come up with a remarkable solution to Kentucky's problems. If Etcovitch would switch off its traffic signals and have a fireman direct traffic, just think of how much money would be saved. They're going to test this asinine idea next Monday through Friday, so we'll need them switched off by (but please, not before!) Sunday night.

Thanks for helping out. If you can arrange it so that we'll have the traffic signals until the last minute, it'll be great. They have to be turned off at all stations; they can't just test one.

If we can be of any help to you, let us know.

Respectfully yours,

Mark: Etcovitch Fire Department.

DISTRICT ATTORNEY

Bizzell County District Attorney
Bizzell County Courthouse
Main Street
Bizzell, NC 28399

Drs. Finklestein, Kirk, Smolin, & Hollis, PA
4500 S. 21st Ave.
Suite 1004
Bizzell, NC 28399

Gentlemen,

In reference to case #549934, City of Bizzell, County of Bizzell, State of North Carolina, we are requesting that the medical records of Henry Jiles be delivered to our office at once.

Your cooperation in this matter is greatly appreciated.

Respectfully yours,

Mark: Bizzell County District Attorney.

Note: This works even better if it is enclosed with a brief cover letter from the doctor and sent to the patient in question. They'll not think that this is very funny. I fell in love with Susan Cieszko, the meanest person that I ever met, and she inspired this letter. Thanks, Susan.

LIBRARY

Pompliano County Library
S Ocean Drive
DiStefano, CA 49800

16 April 1984

Marifino Distributors, Inc.
217 Baynon Rd.
DiStefano, CA 49800

Gentlemen,

We have been allowed $15,000 for duplication equipment. We have analyzed all of the models that meet our specifications and have found your Artiz Model #458L to be the best.

Please deliver as many of this model as our budget will allow within the next 14 days. Our district manager will be on hand and will pay you the full amount in cash as soon as the machines are in place.

Thank you, and we look forward to dealing with you.

Sincerely yours,

Mark: Pompliano County Library.

CORONER

Lussier County Coroner
22 SE 3rd Terr.
Talit, LA 03433

3 March 1984

Schoenthat Memorial Park
708 Windser St.
Talit, LA 03433

Gentlemen,

It has been brought to our attention that you have been engaged in a practice of not making very careful records. In short, your scam is up. We are well aware of your practices.

We aren't amused. We want to know who has been paying you to falsify burial records and we want to know now. If you choose not to speak voluntarily, we will take the following actions against you. We will haul each and every one of you into court on fraud charges. We'll close you down long enough to exhume and positively identify each and every body that is buried on the premises.

We trust that we will be hearing from you within the next 48 hours.

Sincerely yours,

Mark: Lussier County Coroner.

Note: The person who receives this letter should be a fighter who hates the Coroner, too.

SANITATION DEPARTMENT

City of Klarenmayer
Garbage Collection
1400 Main Street
Klarenmayer, Ark 31866

23 December 1984

Klarenmayer Daily Times
1 Press Circle
Klarenmayer, Ark 31860

Gentlemen,

First of all our apologies. This letter should have been in your office a week ago. The drunk who is supposed to handle matters like this was fired yesterday.

As you are aware, we will run a special schedule for the Holiday season.

People who usually have their trash picked up on Mondays will have their trash picked up on Monday, December 24 and Wednesday, December 26. Those who normally have their trash picked up on Tuesdays will have no trash pickup the week of Christmas. Also, Thursday and Friday pickups will be cancelled.

Thank you for informing your readers of this policy. Have a wonderful holiday!

Yours in a clean way,

Mark: City of Klarenmayer Garbage Collection Department.

PROPERTY APPRAISER

Property Appraiser
City of Macaulay, FL
Macaulay, FL 33199

1 April 1984

Mr. J. Petrovich
6500 Federal Rd.
Macaulay, FL 33199

Dear Sir,

I drove by your house yesterday and was most impressed with your addition of a second story. The place really looks sharp.

You neglected to tell us that you had built this addition. It did increase the value of your house, and you had a legal obligation to inform us of it. We have upped the evaluation of your house by 35%. You now owe us an additional $700. If you remit it within the next 3 days we'll just forget about your oversight.

Sincerely yours,

Mark: Macaulay Property Appraiser.

Note: The person who receives this letter hasn't built such an addition.

LICENSING DEPARTMENT

Knowles County Department of Professional Regulation
8975 Hollybrook Road
Binenfield, TX 10043

1 May 1984

Sniderman's
Corner of 5th and 94th Streets
Binenfield, TX 10043

Dear Sir,

We have warned you to clean up your act. The Knowles County Sheriff has warned you to clean up your act. You have choosen to ignore our warnings.

As of this date, your license to serve beer, wine, and food is revoked. You will not be reinstated. If you continue operations, you will be arrested. Hopefully, you'll be arrested anyway.

You have a nice day now.

Respectfully yours,

Mark: Dept. of Licenses.
Note: The meaner the recipients, the better this will work.

DEPARTMENT OF RECREATION

Paglariio Department of Recreation
2301 Lincoln St.
Paglariio, TX 32000

12 May 1984

Mr. Hyrim J. Morse Jr.
106 S. 4th Terr.
Paglariio, TX 32000

Dear Sir,

We realize that the park is a very tempting place to become involved in illicit activities at night. We realize also that this is a serious problem.

We know that morality cannot be legislated. We don't care who you choose to cheat with or on. In the future, however, please do it somewhere else.

If you are caught in the park for any reason after hours you will be arrested for trespass after warning. We're serious. There's a great place on 15th Street that you might want to take your future lovers to.

Sincerely yours,

CC Paglariio Sheriff's Department

Mark: Paglariio Department of Recreation.

Note: Holier-than-thou types make good recipients of this type of letter; they tend to scream loudly. If this type of letter is sent to that type of person, an additional carbon copy should be listed as going to the local newspaper.

PUBLIC SCHOOL SYSTEM

Isenberg County Public Schools
4800 State Road 7
Palacios, Idaho 62001

15 April 1984

DeVincentis Distributors, Inc.
4200 Hillcrest Drive Bay 680
Fleury, Idaho 62221

Gentlemen,

The school board is most pleased with the service that you have provided. Throughout the years, your deliveries to the school cafeterias have been very good.

We are now changing our system. Instead of delivering small quantities to each school, we would like to have everything delivered to our main office (on State Road 7). This will enable us to keep better records, as well as consolidate some of our staff.

Please start delivering your goods to our main office at once. We no longer will accept deliveries at the individual schools.

Respectfully yours,

Mark: Isenberg County Public Schools.

Note: It might be fun to send one of these to each of the school's suppliers. A different location for each supplier should add to the turmoil.

TAX COLLECTOR

Civitano, Inc.
105 N.E. 3rd St.
Rodman, LA 04322

12 September 1984

Rodman Tax Collector
3200 S. Main Street
Rodman, LA 04322

Dear Sir,

Enclosed, please find the final payment of our settlement. It's been three years since I was caught, and let me add that I shan't be caught again.

Enclosed you will find my final certified check, made payable to cash just like all the others, in the amount of $5000.

I sincerely hope that you have grown richer; I haven't.

Sincerely yours,

Mark: City of Rodman Tax Collector.
Note: Do NOT seal this letter. There is no Civitano, Inc.

DEPARTMENT OF ZONING

Rendenille County
Department of Zoning
1400 Raven Street
Suite 1000
Spiro, Kansas 40322

15 June 1984

Spiro Church of God
4800 Harrison Street
Spiro, Kansas 40322

Dear Sir,

In response to several recent complaints, I have investigated the problem that you are causing in reference to parking on Sunday mornings.

Your church is only zoned to park 12 cars, no trucks. Clearly you have been ignoring this regulation. Your neighbors aren't pleased with this.

If you fail to obey this regulation, we shall be forced to have the local gendarmes ticket and/or tow violators, as well as bring charges against your church's management.

Let's end this issue here before it becomes unpleasant for all involved.

Respectfully,

Mark: Rendenille County Department of Zoning.
Note: The local papers would probably like a copy of this one.

ANIMAL CONTROL

City of Hauskins
Animal Control
610 N.W. 66th Ter.
Fort Haynick, Tenn 73220

19 April 1984

Mr. H.D. Parmet
1400 S.W. 45 St.
Fort Haynick, Tenn 73220

Dear Sir,

City ordinance 3945 requires that all animals have proper registration if they are housed within the city. It further mandates that a $100.00 fine be levied against those who will not comply.

You have failed to heed our warnings. We have sent you letters on three occasions in reference to your failure to comply. If you choose to make a donation in the sum of $100.00 to the Humane Society, we will not press this matter. If, however, you choose to ignore this letter too, you will be arrested and tried.

Sincerely,

Mark: City of Hauskins Animal Control.

Note: Mr. Parmet doesn't have a dog, nor has he received such letters before. Should I say that he won't make a donation?

HIGHWAY PATROL

Highway Patrol Division 8
6971 Lee Drive
Shanley, Alaska 43333

14 April 1984

Spucy County Elementary School
6225 Dewey Rd.
Krasun, Alaska 43334

Gentlemen,

We will have one of our officers at your school on April 28 at 10:00 AM to give a presentation entitled "Safety and You." It is a two hour presentation and is geared for school aged children.

This is, of course, part of the governor's safety program.

We won't need anything from you except a place to plug in our slide projector.

We'll see you April 28.

Sincerely yours,

Mark: Highway Patrol.
Note: Don't you hate somebody who lies to kids? This one is a real image breaker.

DIVISION OF DRIVERS LICENSES

L.K. Michaels
619 E. 49th St.
Hapern, PA 42003

19 April 1984

Department of Licenses
7400 Grant Circle
Graham, PA 42014

Gentlemen,

On 18 March 1984 I mailed my restoration fee to your office. I received my cancelled check three weeks later. I have yet to receive my license back.

I did everything that the clerk in your Anderson County office told me to do.

Please rush this; three months of lost driving is enough punishment for any man.

Sincerely yours,

L.K. Michaels

Mark: Department of Licenses.

Note: Mr. Michaels didn't write this letter. I'd be willing to bet that he writes one when the Division of Licenses "replies."

CLERK OF COURT

Kirby County Clerk of Court
Kirby County Courthouse
Cogan, OK 56300

12 July 1984

Mr. E. J. Palos
Palos, Robins, Miller & Williams, PA
1400 S. Hampton Drive
Cogan, OK 56300

Dear Gene,

We need you to drop by the office Saturday morning at 7:00 AM. Judge Kitt is going over the records (he likes to do that sort of thing) and needs you for clarification.

It seems that some of the records have been lost. We are calling in all of the people who work with Judge Kitt and compiling these missing records the best we can. You just happened to draw Saturday morning.

We'll see you Saturday.

Respectfullly,

Mark: Kirby County Courthouse Clerk of Court.

AFTERWARD

You've read the last letter, but it's really only the first. There are countless uses for each of the letters in this book. A little creativity is all it takes.

I've told you how to stay safe. I've told you how to obtain postmarks hundreds of miles away. I've told you how to obtain letterheads. I have not suggested that you actually try any of these scams; the person who buys this kind of book already knows better.

I really hope that you have enjoyed this book. If you have some ideas that you think would go well in Volume 2, send them to me in care of KMIC (their address is in my introductory remarks). I love a good laugh.

Happy revenge to you. Remember the definition of revenge and you'll go far. You can't ruin a deserving mark; he ruins himself. Until Volume II, have fun and stay nasty.

YOU WILL ALSO WANT TO READ:

☐ **55083 Espionage: Down & Dirty,** *by Tony Lesce.* What's spying really like? Read this book and find out. Covers recruiting, training, infiltration, payment (including sex), evacuation, what happens when a spy is exposed, and more. Also reveals the exploits of many notorious spies: The Walker Spy Ring, "Falcon and Snowman," the Pollard Case, and many others. *1991, 5½ x 8½, 180 pp, soft cover.* $17.95.

☐ **19169 Take No Prisoners, Destroying Enemies with Dirty and Malicious Tricks,** *by Mack Nasty.* Mack Nasty doesn't believe in holding a grudge. He believes in swift, sure and *devastating* retribution. In this book, Mack reveals the most deliciously despicable revenge techniques ever conceived. How to destroy you enemy's house or car. How to get someone arrested for drug trafficking, kiddie porn, firearms violations or product tampering. *Sold for entertainment purposes only. 1990, 5½ x 8½, 118 pp, soft cover.* $10.00.

☐ **55072 The Muckraker's Manual, How To Do Your Own Investigative Reporting,** *by M. Harry.* How to dig out the dirt on anyone! Written for investigative reporters exposing political corruption, the detailed professional investigative techniques are useful to any investigation. Developing "inside" sources; Getting documents; Incredible ruses that really work; Interviewing techniques; Infiltration; When to stop an investigation; Protecting your sources; And much more. *1984, 5½ x 8½, 148 pp, illustrated, soft cover.* $12.95.

And much, much more! We offer the very finest in controversial and unusual books — please turn to our catalog ad on the next page.

**LOOMPANICS UNLIMITED
PO BOX 1197
PORT TOWNSEND, WA 98368**

PPL94

Please send me the titles I have checked above. I have enclosed $_____ which includes $4.00 for the shipping and handling of 1 to 3 books, $6.00 for 4 or more.

Name _____

Address _____

City _____

State/Zip _____
(Washington residents please include 7.9% sales tax.)

"Loompanics is visionary..."
— Village Voice

"Books that test the First Amendment the way a bad child tests a permissive parent."
— The Orlando Sentinel

"Fully indexed, graphically laid out, the Loompanics catalog is a real shopping trip. And well worth it... a natural for small press people."
— Small Press Review

"An astonishing line of books..."
— The Washington Post

"Here are books that are very definitely *not* at your local library or bookstore."
— The Whole Earth Catalog

"Loompanics is probably the most radical catalog and press of all....."
— City Paper

"Scary..."
— Publisher's Weekly

"Serving millions of fringe info-gatherers daily... Loompanics Unlimited is the Looney Tunes of totally cool texts... the hepcats of out-there-lit."
— Spin

THE BEST BOOK CATALOG IN THE WORLD!!!

We offer hard-to-find books on the world's most unusual subjects. Here are a few of the topics covered IN DEPTH in our exciting new catalog:

- *Hiding/Concealment of physical objects! A complete section of the best books ever written on hiding things.*
- *Fake ID/Alternate Identities! The most comprehensive selection of books on this little-known subject ever offered for sale! You have to see it to believe it!*
- *Investigative/Undercover methods and techniques! Professional secrets known only to a few, now revealed to you to use! Actual police manuals on shadowing and surveillance!*
- *And much, much more, including Locks and Lockpicking, Self-Defense, Intelligence Increase, Life Extension, Money-Making Opportunities, Human Oddities, Exotic Weapons, Sex, Drugs, Anarchism, and more!*

Our book catalog is 280 pages, 8½ x 11, packed with over 800 of the most controversial and unusual books ever printed! You can order every book listed! Periodic supplements keep you posted on the LATEST titles available!!! Our catalog is $5.00, including shipping and handling.

Our book catalog is truly THE BEST BOOK CATALOG IN THE WORLD! Order yours today. You will be very pleased, we know.

LOOMPANICS UNLIMITED
PO BOX 1197
PORT TOWNSEND, WA 98368
(206) 385-2230

Name _____

Address _____

City/State/Zip _____
Now accepting Visa and MasterCard.